Finding Healing: Navigating the Pain of Marriage through Biblical Wisdom

"Embracing Transformation and Renewal in the Journey of Marriage"

MUZI KHUMALO

Dedication

This book is dedicated to every man who has ever felt the weight of marital pain, who has wrestled with doubt, fear, and uncertainty in the depths of his heart. It is dedicated to those who have dared to hope for healing, for restoration, and for a brighter tomorrow.

To the husbands who have weathered storms and stood by their wives through thick and thin, this book is for you. Your strength, your resilience, and your unwavering commitment to your marriage inspire us all.

To the fathers who have set an example of love, sacrifice, and dedication for their children to follow, this book is for you. Your legacy of faith, integrity, and compassion will echo through the generations to come. To the sons who are just beginning their own journeys of love and commitment, this book is for you. May the lessons learned from the pain of the past guide you, strengthen you, and shape you into the husbands and fathers you are called to be.

And finally, to the one who holds all things together to God, the author and perfecter of our faith this book is dedicated. May His love, His grace, and His faithfulness sustain you on your journey, and may His presence be a constant source of strength and comfort in the midst of life's trials and tribulations.

With gratitude and humility, we offer this book as a testament to the power of hope, the beauty of redemption, and the transformative nature of love. May it serve as a beacon of light and encouragement on your journey toward a thriving and fulfilling marriage, and may you always remember that with God, all things are possible.

"Though one may be overpowered, two can defend themselves. A cord of three strands is not quickly broken."
— Ecclesiastes 4:12, KJV

"And above all things have fervent charity among yourselves: for charity shall cover the multitude of sins."
— 1 Peter 4:8, KJV

"And above all these things put on charity, which is the bond of perfectness."
— Colossians 3:14, KJV

"The Lord is nigh unto them that are of a broken heart; and saveth such as be of a contrite spirit."
— Psalm 34:18, KJV

"Charity suffereth long, and is kind; charity envieth not; charity vaunteth not itself, is not puffed up, Doth not behave itself unseemly, seeketh not her own, is not easily provoked, thinketh no evil;"
— 1 Corinthians 13:4-5, KJV

Contents

Title Page

Copyright

Dedication

Epigraph

Foreword

Introduction

Preface

Prologue

Untitled

Chapter 1:

Chapter 2:

Chapter 3:

Chapter 4:

Chapter 6:

Chapter 7:

Chapter 5:

Chapter 8:

Epilogue: Hope for the Journey Ahead

Acknowledgement

<u>About The Author</u>

<u>About The Author</u>

Foreword

It is with great pleasure and a deep sense of honor that I pen these words for Pastor Muzi Khumalo's remarkable work, "Finding Healing: Navigating the Pain of Marriage through Biblical Wisdom." As a scholar of the Word and a committed servant in the ministry, I have had the privilege of witnessing the profound impact that sound biblical teaching can have on the lives of individuals and families. Pastor Khumalo's book is a testament to this transformative power.

Marriage, as we know, is a sacred covenant that joins two hearts in a journey of love and companionship. However, it is also a path fraught with challenges and trials that can often lead to profound pain and disillusionment. In an era where the complexities of marital life can be overwhelming, Pastor Khumalo offers a beacon of hope through his thoughtful and faith-driven insights.

In this book, Pastor Khumalo addresses the often hidden and unspoken struggles that many face within their marriages. With a compassionate heart and a keen understanding of both the spiritual and practical aspects of marriage, he delves into the root causes of marital pain and provides a biblical framework for healing and restoration.

The chapters are carefully crafted to guide readers through a journey of understanding and healing, beginning with a deep exploration of marital pain and moving through to the practical application of biblical wisdom in addressing these challenges. Pastor Khumalo's ability to weave together scriptural insights with practical advice offers a holistic approach to marital healing.

As the Bishop of the International Missions Centre (IMC) Eswatini, I have seen firsthand the impact that a strong, faith-centered approach can have on relationships. Pastor Khumalo's work not only resonates with the timeless truths of Scripture but also provides actionable steps that can help couples navigate the rough waters of marital conflict and find a renewed sense of connection and purpose.

"Finding Healing" is more than just a book; it is a guide for those who seek to deepen their understanding of marital pain and find a path toward restoration. It is an invaluable resource for couples who are struggling and for those who wish to strengthen their relationship through faith and perseverance.

I commend Pastor Muzi Khumalo for his dedication to addressing these vital issues and for his commitment to providing a resource that is both spiritually enriching and practically useful. May this book serve as a source of encouragement and transformation for many, leading them to experience the fullness of healing and renewal that God desires for their marriages.

With sincere blessings,

Dr. Samuel Dlamini

Book Writer and Scholar of the Word

Bishop of International Missions Centre (IMC) Eswatini, Manzini.

Introduction

Marriage is a journey of love, companionship, and shared dreams. It is a sacred bond that unites two souls in a covenant of commitment and devotion. Yet, amidst the beauty and joy of married life, there are also moments of pain, struggle, and heartache.

For many men, the pain of marriage can be a deeply personal and often silent burden. Whether it's the weight of unmet expectations, the sting of unresolved conflicts, or the ache of loneliness in the midst of intimacy, the sources of marital pain are varied and complex. And while societal expectations may dictate that men remain stoic and strong, the reality is that the pain exists, and it can take a toll on both individuals and relationships.

In this book, we delve into the hidden depths of marital pain, exploring its sources, its impact, and its transformative potential. Drawing from the timeless wisdom of Scripture, as well as insights from modern psychology and personal experiences, we offer a beacon of hope and encouragement on the journey toward healing and restoration.

But this book is not merely a roadmap for navigating the challenges of marriage – it is also a call to action, a call to embrace vulnerability, humility, and grace in our relationships. It is a reminder that no matter how deep the pain may be, there is always hope – hope for healing, hope for renewal, and hope for a brighter future.

As we embark on this journey together, may we do so with open hearts, willing to confront the pain of the past and embrace the possibility of a new beginning. May we find comfort in the knowledge that we are not alone, that there is a community of support waiting to walk alongside us on the path toward healing and restoration.

And may we hold fast to the promise that with faith, perseverance, and a willingness to seek help when needed, anything is possible. For in the midst of our pain, there is also the opportunity for growth, transformation, and a deeper understanding of ourselves and our spouses.

So, as we turn the page to the next chapter of our journey, let us do so with courage, with hope, and with a steadfast belief that the best is yet to come. For the journey ahead may be challenging, but it is also filled with endless possibilities for growth, transformation, and joy. And with God as our guide and love as our compass, we can navigate the waters of marriage with grace, resilience, and unwavering hope.

Preface

In the quiet moments of reflection, amidst the hustle and bustle of daily life, there exists a profound truth marriage is both a journey and a destination.

It is a sacred union between two souls, a covenant of love, commitment, and companionship that transcends the boundaries of time and space. But like any journey worth embarking upon, marriage is not without its challenges, its trials, and its moments of pain.

As a man navigating the complexities of marriage, you may find yourself grappling with feelings of loneliness, frustration, or disillusionment. You may wonder if you are alone in your struggles, if your pain is unique, if there is any hope for healing and restoration. It is for you, dear reader, that this book is written.

In the pages that follow, we delve into the hidden depths of marital pain, exploring its sources, its impact, and its transformative potential. Drawing from the timeless wisdom of Scripture, as well as insights from modern psychology and personal experiences, we offer a beacon of hope and encouragement on your journey toward a thriving and fulfilling marriage.

From the biblical perspective on marriage to the transformative power of forgiveness, from the role of community and support networks to the importance of embracing growth and transformation, each chapter is crafted with care and intentionality to provide you with practical insights, actionable strategies, and a renewed sense of hope.

But this book is not merely a roadmap for navigating the challenges of marriage – it is also a call to action, a call to embrace vulnerability, humility, and grace in your relationships. It is a reminder that no matter how deep the pain may be, there is always hope – hope for healing, hope for renewal, and hope for a brighter future.

Prologue

arriage is a tapestry woven with threads of love, joy, companionship, and shared dreams. It is a sacred bond that unites two souls in a covenant of commitment and devotion, embarking on a journey of mutual growth and fulfillment. However, alongside the beauty and joy of married life, there are moments of pain, struggle, and heartache that many couples endure in silence.

For countless men, the pain of marriage can be a deeply personal and often unspoken burden. It might be the weight of unmet expectations, the sting of unresolved conflicts, or the profound ache of loneliness even in the presence of a spouse. Society often expects men to remain stoic and strong, masking their struggles behind a facade of resilience. But beneath this exterior, the reality of marital pain exists, taking a toll on both individuals and relationships.

"Finding Healing: Navigating the Pain of Marriage through Biblical Wisdom" seeks to illuminate these hidden struggles, offering a path toward understanding, healing, and transformation. This book is a heartfelt exploration of the sources of marital pain, their impact, and the transformative potential that lies within these challenging experiences. By drawing from the timeless wisdom of Scripture, modern psychological insights, and personal stories, it aims to provide hope and encouragement to those navigating the complexities of married life.

This journey is not just about recognizing the pain; it is about finding healing and restoration. It is about embracing vulnerability, humility, and grace in our relationships. It is a call to action, urging us to confront the pain of the past and to embrace the possibility of a new beginning. Through faith, perseverance, and the support of a loving community, we can find the strength to heal and the courage to transform our marriages.

As you embark on this journey with us, may you do so with an open heart and a willing spirit. May you find comfort in knowing that you are not alone and that there is a community ready to walk alongside you. Hold fast to the promise that with God as your guide and love as your compass, the journey ahead, though challenging, is filled with endless possibilities for growth, transformation, and joy.

Let us turn the page and begin this journey together, with hope, courage, and an unwavering belief that the best is yet to come. For in the depths of our pain lies the potential for profound healing and transformation, leading us to a deeper understanding of ourselves, our spouses, and the sacred bond of marriage.

Untitled

Chapter 1:

The Hidden Depths of Marital Pain

Objectives:

1. Illuminate Sources: Explore reasons for marital pain, like unmet expectations and communication breakdown, to help readers understand the complexities.

> Ephisian 4:26-27
> 1 Corinthians 14:4-7

2. Offer Insight: Combine biblical teachings and psychology to provide practical strategies for healing and growth.

> James 1:2-4
> Romans 12:2

3. Encourage Connection: Share relatable stories to show readers they're not alone and that there's hope for restoration.

Ecclesiastes 4:9-10

Galatians 6:2

Goals:

1. Raise Awareness: Highlight the overlooked issue of marital pain and foster empathy

1Peter 5:7

Proverb 15:22

2. Provide Guidance: Equip readers with practical tools for communication, conflict resolution, and seeking support.

Proverb 15:1

Matthew 18:15

3. Inspire Transformation: Encourage readers to see marital pain as an opportunity for growth and renewal.

Romans 8:28

2Corinthians 4:16

Definition:

"The Hidden Depths of Marital Pain" refers to the emotional struggles in marriage, like unmet needs and unresolved conflicts that can lead to feelings of loneliness and frustration. Despite its challenges, marital pain can lead to growth and renewal when approached with openness and grace, as seen in Scripture.

$$\infty \, \infty \, \infty$$

In the quiet corners of many marriages, there lies a silent struggle the pain that often goes unspoken. For men, this pain can be particularly acute, yet societal expectations often dictate that they remain stoic, burying their feelings deep within. But the truth is, the pain exists, and it can erode the very foundation of a marriage if left unaddressed.

Marriage is a sacred union ordained by God, designed to be a source of love, companionship, and mutual support.

However, in the fallen world we inhabit, marriages are often marred by pain and brokenness. Men, in particular, may find themselves grappling with the weight of unspoken burdens, feeling the pressure to maintain an image of strength and control even when they are hurting inside.

Yet, the Bible acknowledges the reality of pain within marriage and offers words of comfort and guidance to those who are struggling.

In 1 Peter 3:7, husbands are urged to treat their wives with understanding, recognizing them as fellow heirs of the grace of life. This verse reminds us that marriage is a partnership, and that understanding and empathy are essential ingredients for a healthy relationship.

Similarly, Ephesians 4:26-27 cautions against allowing unresolved anger to fester within marriage: "In your anger do not sin: Do not let the sun go down while you are still angry, and do not give the devil a foothold."

This passage emphasizes the importance of addressing conflicts and grievances in a timely manner, lest they give rise to bitterness and division within the marriage.

The pain experienced within marriage is often multifaceted, stemming from a variety of sources such as unmet expectations, communication breakdowns, and unresolved conflicts. Proverbs 13:12 speaks to the anguish caused by deferred hope: "Hope deferred makes the heart sick, but a longing fulfilled is a tree of life."

When expectations go unmet and hopes are dashed, it can leave a deep sense of disappointment and disillusionment in its wake.

Furthermore, the pressure to conform to societal norms and expectations can exacerbate the pain experienced within marriage.

Men may feel the weight of cultural stereotypes that dictate they must be strong, stoic, and emotionally invulnerable at all times. Yet, Ecclesiastes 4:9-10 reminds us of the value of companionship and support: "Two are better than one, because they have a good return for their labor: If either of them falls down, one can help the other up. But pity anyone who falls and has no one to help them up."

In the midst of marital pain, men may find themselves struggling to reconcile their faith with their circumstances.

They may question God's plan for their marriage and wonder if their pain is a reflection of divine disfavor. Yet, Romans 8:28 offers reassurance that God works all things together for the good of those who love Him: "And we know that in all things God works for the good of those who love him, who have been called according to his purpose."

Even in the midst of pain and adversity, God is at work, weaving together a beautiful tapestry of redemption and restoration.

Acknowledging the existence of marital pain is the first step towards healing. Men must resist the temptation to bury their feelings or downplay their struggles, instead allowing themselves to fully experience and express their emotions.

Psalm 34:18 reminds us that God is close to the brokenhearted: "The Lord is close to the brokenhearted and saves those who are crushed in spirit." God invites us to bring our pain and brokenness to Him, knowing that He is a compassionate and loving Father who longs to comfort and restore His children.

In the subsequent chapters, we will delve deeper into the sources of marital pain and explore practical strategies for finding healing and restoration.

Through honest communication, mutual understanding, and a willingness to seek help when needed, men can begin to navigate the complexities of marital pain with faith and resilience.

Chapter 2:

Unveiling the Sources of Marital Pain

Objectives:

1. Identify Sources: Explain various causes of marital pain, like unmet expectations and communication issues, to help readers understand their marital struggles better.

>Ephesians 4:26-27
>
>1 Corinthians 13:4-7

Goals:

1. Increase Awareness: Help readers recognize potential areas of marital struggle by highlighting common sources of pain in marriage.

>Proverbs 15:1
>
>James 1:19

Definition:

"Unveiling the Sources of Marital Pain" involves understanding and addressing the root causes of marital struggles to foster healthier relationships.

∞ ∞ ∞

Marital pain is often a result of various underlying issues that can strain the relationship between spouses. From unmet expectations to communication breakdowns, from unresolved conflicts to the weight of responsibilities, the triggers for marital pain are indeed varied and complex. In this chapter, we will delve into these issues, shining a light on the underlying causes that often plague marriages.

One significant source of marital pain is unmet expectations. Each spouse enters into marriage with their own set of hopes, dreams, and desires, often shaped by their upbringing, past experiences, and cultural influences.

When these expectations are not communicated or aligned with those of their partner, it can lead to feelings of disappointment, frustration, and resentment.

Proverbs 13:12 aptly describes the anguish that comes from deferred hope: "Hope deferred makes the heart sick, but a longing fulfilled is a tree of life." Unmet expectations can indeed leave the heart feeling sick and weary.

Communication breakdowns also play a significant role in marital pain. Effective communication is the lifeblood of any healthy relationship, yet many couples struggle to express their thoughts, feelings, and needs in a constructive manner.

Proverbs 18:21 reminds us of the power of words: "The tongue has the power of life and death, and those who love it will eat its fruit." Hurtful words spoken in the heat of the moment can inflict deep wounds that take time to heal, contributing to ongoing pain within the marriage.

Moreover, unresolved conflicts can create a breeding ground for marital pain. Every marriage experiences disagreements and disagreements, but when these conflicts are left unresolved or swept under the rug, they can fester and grow, eroding the trust and intimacy between spouses. Ephesians 4:26-27 urges us not to let anger linger unresolved: "In your anger do not sin: Do not let the sun go down while you are still angry, and do not give the devil a foothold."

Addressing conflicts in a timely and respectful manner is essential for maintaining a healthy and thriving marriage.

The weight of responsibilities can also contribute to marital pain, particularly in today's fast-paced and demanding world.

From juggling work commitments to managing household duties to caring for children, spouses may find themselves feeling overwhelmed and burnt out. Galatians 6:2 encourages us to bear one another's burdens: "Carry each other's burdens, and in this way, you will fulfill the law of Christ."

When spouses feel supported and valued, they are better able to navigate the challenges of life together.

Financial struggles, infidelity, addiction, and differences in values or beliefs are additional sources of marital pain that can deeply impact the health and stability of a marriage.

However, regardless of the specific issues couples may face, the key to overcoming marital pain lies in addressing these issues with honesty, humility, and a willingness to seek help when needed.

In the subsequent chapters, we will explore how couples can navigate these sources of marital pain with wisdom and grace, drawing upon both biblical principles and practical insights to strengthen their relationship and find healing and restoration.

Through open communication, mutual respect, and a commitment to working through challenges together, couples can build a marriage that withstands the tests of time and adversity.

∞ ∞ ∞

Chapter 3:

The Biblical Perspective on Marriage

Objectives:

1. Explore Divine Intentions: Look into what the Bible says about marriage, focusing on love, commitment, and respect as its core values.

- Genesis 2:24
- Ephesians 5:25

2. Offer Practical Wisdom: Share practical advice from Scripture on love, forgiveness, and perseverance to help readers understand their roles in marriage better.

- Colossians 3:14
- 1 Peter 4:8

1. Inspire Reflection: Encourage readers to think about their marriages in light of biblical teachings, recognizing the significance and purpose of their union.

- Proverbs 18:22
- Hebrews 13:4

Definition:

"The Biblical Perspective on Marriage" involves understanding marriage according to the Bible, emphasizing its sacredness and offering practical guidance for couples to live out biblical principles in their relationships.

∞∞∞

I n the midst of pain and turmoil within marriage, men can find solace and guidance in the timeless wisdom of the Bible.

The Scriptures offer profound insights into the divine intention behind the sacred union of marriage, providing a framework for understanding, navigating, and ultimately transforming the challenges that couples may face.

From the pages of Scripture, we glean wisdom on love, forgiveness, patience, and perseverance all essential ingredients for a thriving marriage.

At the heart of the biblical perspective on marriage lies the recognition of its divine origin and purpose. In Genesis 2:24, we read: "Therefore a man shall leave his father and his mother and hold fast to his wife, and they shall become one flesh."

This verse highlights the unity and intimacy that God intended for marriage from the beginning a union that transcends mere physical or emotional connection and encompasses a deep, spiritual bond between husband and wife.

Love is a central theme in the Bible's portrayal of marriage. In Ephesians 5:25, husbands are called to love their wives sacrificially, just as Christ loved the church and gave Himself up for her.

This selfless, sacrificial love mirrors the love that Christ has for His people and serves as a model for husbands in their relationship with their wives. Similarly, Titus 2:4 encourages wives to love their husbands and children, emphasizing the importance of nurturing and cultivating love within the family.

Forgiveness is another foundational principle of biblical marriage. In Colossians 3:13, we are urged to bear with one another and forgive whatever grievances we may have against one another, just as the Lord forgave us.

This verse reminds us that forgiveness is not merely a virtue but a commandment a necessary component of maintaining healthy relationships and fostering reconciliation and healing.

Patience and perseverance are also essential qualities for navigating the challenges of marriage. In Galatians 6:9, we are encouraged not to grow weary in doing good, for in due season we will reap a harvest if we do not give up. This verse reminds us of the importance of perseverance in the face of adversity, trusting in God's faithfulness and provision even when the road seems long and difficult.

Furthermore, the Bible offers practical wisdom for building and maintaining a strong and healthy marriage. In Proverbs 15:1, we are reminded of the power of gentle words to diffuse conflict and restore harmony: "A gentle answer turns away wrath, but a harsh word stirs up anger." Similarly, Proverbs 18:22 extols the value of finding a wife who is a true partner and companion: "He who finds a wife finds what is good and receives favor from the Lord."

In times of marital pain and struggle, men can turn to the Scriptures for comfort, guidance, and inspiration. Through prayer, study, and meditation on God's Word, husbands can find strength and wisdom to navigate the complexities of marriage with grace and humility.

By embodying the principles of love, forgiveness, patience, and perseverance found in the Bible, men can cultivate a marriage that reflects the beauty and sanctity of God's design.

In the subsequent chapters, we will explore how men can apply these biblical principles to their marriages, drawing upon the timeless wisdom of Scripture to find healing, restoration, and renewed intimacy with their spouses.

With faith as our guide and the Word of God as our foundation, we embark on a journey towards a thriving and fulfilling marriage that honors God and blesses those around us.

Chapter 4:

Finding Healing Through Faith

Objectives:

1. Discover Spiritual Strength: Explore how faith can bring comfort and resilience during marital struggles.

- Psalm 34:18
- Isaiah 41:10

2. Encourage Prayer: Promote prayer as a way to find guidance and peace in difficult times.

- Philippians 4:6-7
- James 5:16

Goals:

1. Provide Spiritual Support: Offer encouragement to readers to deepen their faith and find healing through prayer.

- Psalm 147:3
- Jeremiah 17:14

Definition:

"Finding Healing Through Faith" means seeking emotional and spiritual healing in marriage by relying on one's faith for strength and guidance. It emphasizes the power of prayer and trust in God's ability to heal and restore.

∞∞∞

In times of distress, when the weight of marital pain feels overwhelming, faith can serve as a beacon of hope, guiding men towards healing and restoration.

Drawing from the rich tapestry of biblical stories and teachings, we embark on a journey of exploration into how faith can be a transformative force in marriages.

Whether it's through prayer, seeking counsel from wise mentors, or engaging in spiritual practices, faith has the power to renew, heal, and strengthen relationships.

At the heart of faith is trust – trust in a loving and faithful God who walks alongside us in our trials and tribulations. In Psalm

46:1, we are reminded that "God is our refuge and strength, an ever-present help in trouble."

This verse speaks to the unwavering support and comfort that God offers to His children, even in the darkest of times. By placing our trust in Him, we can find the courage to confront our pain and seek healing for our marriages.

Prayer is a powerful tool for cultivating faith and finding solace in times of distress. In Philippians 4:6-7, we are encouraged to present our requests to God with thanksgiving, knowing that He hears and responds to our prayers: "Do not be anxious about anything, but in every situation, by prayer and petition, with thanksgiving, present your requests to God. And the peace of God, which transcends all understanding, will guard your hearts and your minds in Christ Jesus." Through prayer, we can pour out our hearts to God, seeking His guidance, comfort, and wisdom for our marriages.

Seeking counsel from wise mentors and spiritual leaders can also be instrumental in finding healing and restoration in marriage. Proverbs 11:14 tells us, "Where there is no guidance, a people falls, but in an abundance of counselors there is safety."

Trusted mentors and counselors can offer valuable insights, perspectives, and encouragement, helping men navigate the complexities of marital pain with grace and wisdom. By humbly seeking counsel from others, men can gain clarity and direction for their journey towards healing.

Furthermore, engaging in spiritual practices such as meditation, worship, and fasting can deepen our connection with God and strengthen our faith. In Isaiah 40:31, we are reminded that "those who hope in the Lord will renew their strength. They will soar on wings like eagles; they will run and not grow weary, they will walk and not be faint."

Through spiritual disciplines, we can cultivate a sense of inner peace, resilience, and perseverance, enabling us to withstand the storms of life and emerge stronger and more resilient.

The Bible is replete with stories of individuals who found healing and restoration through their faith in God. The story of Job serves as a powerful reminder of God's sovereignty and faithfulness in the midst of suffering.

Despite enduring unimaginable loss and pain, Job remained steadfast in his faith, declaring, "Though he slay me, yet will I hope in him" (Job 13:15). Job's unwavering trust in God ultimately led to his restoration and blessing.

Similarly, the story of Joseph illustrates how God can bring beauty from ashes and redemption from brokenness. Sold into slavery by his own brothers and unjustly imprisoned, Joseph endured years of hardship and adversity.

Yet, through it all, he remained faithful to God, trusting in His sovereign plan. In the end, God elevated Joseph to a position of authority and used him to save his family and countless others from famine.

These biblical narratives serve as poignant reminders that no matter how dire our circumstances may seem, God is always at work behind the scenes, orchestrating redemption and restoration.

By placing our trust in Him and leaning on His promises, we can find hope, healing, and renewal for our marriages.

In conclusion, faith is a powerful catalyst for transformation in marriage. Through prayer, seeking counsel, and engaging in spiritual practices, men can find healing and restoration in the midst of marital pain. By placing their trust in God and His unfailing love, they can navigate the challenges of marriage with grace, resilience, and hope.

As they draw near to God, He will draw near to them, offering comfort, strength, and renewal for their journey ahead.

Chapter 6:

The Role of Community and Support

Objectives:

1. Highlight Importance: Stress the significance of having a supportive community in facing marital challenges, fostering strength and growth.

- Ecclesiastes 4:12
- Galatians 6:2

Goals:

1. Encourage Seeking Help: Advocate for seeking guidance from trusted individuals or support groups to reduce isolation and promote healing.

- Proverbs 11:14
- James 5:16

"The Role of Community and Support" means recognizing the value of outside relationships in helping couples overcome marital difficulties and find healing and growth.

$$\infty \infty \infty$$

"No man is an island," wrote the poet *John Donne,* and nowhere is this sentiment more apparent than in the context of marriage.

Navigating the challenges and complexities of married life alone can be overwhelming, but with the support of a strong community, couples can find comfort, guidance, and strength to overcome even the most daunting obstacles.

In this chapter, we explore the vital role that community and support networks play in overcoming marital pain, drawing from both biblical principles and modern insights.

From its inception, the Bible emphasizes the importance of community and mutual support in the journey of faith. In Ecclesiastes 4:9-10, we read, "Two are better than one because they have a good return for their labor: If either of them falls down, one can help the other up. But pity anyone who falls and has no one to help them up."

This verse underscores the value of companionship and solidarity, highlighting the strength that comes from walking alongside others in times of need.

The concept of community is central to the Christian faith, as exemplified by the early church described in the book of Acts. Acts 2:42-47 paints a vivid picture of a vibrant and supportive community of believers who "devoted themselves to the apostles' teaching and to fellowship, to the breaking of bread and to prayer."

This community shared their resources, supported one another in times of need, and celebrated together in times of joy.

In the same way, couples can find encouragement and support within the context of their faith community, whether it be through a small group, church family, or fellowship of believers.

In addition to spiritual community, seeking professional help when needed can also play a crucial role in overcoming marital pain. Proverbs 15:22 advises, "Plans fail for lack of counsel, but with many advisers, they succeed."

Just as seeking wise counsel is important in other areas of life, so too is it important in marriage. Professional counselors, therapists, and marriage mentors can offer valuable insights, perspectives, and strategies for navigating the challenges of marriage and finding healing and restoration.

Moreover, participating in marriage enrichment programs and workshops can provide couples with tools and resources for strengthening their relationship and deepening their connection.

These programs often offer practical skills training, opportunities for reflection and discussion, and support from other couples who are facing similar challenges.

By investing in their relationship and prioritizing growth and development, couples can lay a solid foundation for a healthy and thriving marriage.

Support networks also play a vital role in providing emotional support and validation for couples experiencing marital pain.

Simply having a safe space to share their struggles and receive empathy and encouragement can be incredibly healing. Romans 12:15 encourages us to "Rejoice with those who rejoice; mourn with those who mourn."

This verse reminds us of the importance of empathy and solidarity in supporting one another through life's joys and sorrows.

Furthermore, couples can benefit from the wisdom and experience of older, more seasoned couples who have weathered the storms of marriage and emerged stronger and more resilient. Titus 2:3-5 speaks to the value of intergenerational mentorship within the faith community: "Likewise, teach the older women to be reverent in the way they live, not to be slanderers or addicted to much wine, but to teach what is good.

Then they can urge the younger women to love their husbands and children, to be self-controlled and pure, to be busy at home, to be kind, and to be subject to their husbands, so that no one will malign the word of God."

By learning from the experiences and insights of those who have gone before them, couples can gain valuable wisdom and guidance for their own journey.

In conclusion, the role of community and support in overcoming marital pain cannot be overstated. From the biblical concept of community to the importance of seeking professional help when needed, couples can find strength, encouragement, and guidance in their journey towards healing and restoration.

By surrounding themselves with a supportive network of friends, family, mentors, and professionals, couples can weather the storms of marriage with grace, resilience, and hope. Together, they are stronger.

Chapter 7:

Forgiveness and Restoration

Objectives:

1. Explore Forgiveness: Look at the importance of forgiving within marriage for healing and repairing relationships.
- Colossians 3:13
- Matthew 6:14-15

2. Promote Restoration: Discuss ways to rebuild trust and reconcile after conflicts, focusing on renewal and moving forward.
- 2 Corinthians 5:17
- Ephesians 4:32

Goals:

1. Encourage Forgiveness: Encourage readers to forgive to release resentment and foster reconciliation.

• Matthew 18:21-22

2. Facilitate Restoration: Provide practical guidance on restoring relationships and rebuilding trust.
• Romans 12:18

Definition:

"Forgiveness and Restoration" means letting go of past hurts, reconciling differences, and rebuilding trust in marriage, guided by biblical principles.

∞ ∞ ∞

Forgiveness is a cornerstone of healthy relationships, both in the context of marriage and beyond. It is not merely a virtue but a transformative act that has the power to heal wounds, mend brokenness, and restore relationships to wholeness.

In this chapter, we delve into the profound significance of forgiveness, exploring its transformative power in the context of marriage and drawing insights from both biblical teachings and modern psychology.

The Bible is replete with teachings on forgiveness, emphasizing its central importance in the life of faith. Ephesians 4:32 exhorts us to "Be kind and compassionate to one another, forgiving each other, just as in Christ God forgave you."

This verse underscores the profound connection between the forgiveness we receive from God and the forgiveness we extend to others.

Just as we have been forgiven by God, so too are we called to forgive others including our spouses with kindness and compassion.

Jesus Himself modeled radical forgiveness throughout His ministry, demonstrating a willingness to extend grace and mercy even to those who had wronged Him.

In Matthew 18:21-22, Peter asked Jesus, "Lord, how many times shall I forgive my brother or sister who sins against me? Up to seven times?" Jesus replied, "I tell you, not seven times, but seventy-seven times."

This passage highlights the limitless nature of forgiveness, challenging us to cultivate a spirit of forgiveness that knows no bounds.

Forgiveness is not always easy, especially in the context of marriage where wounds can run deep and emotions can run high. However, the act of forgiveness is not merely for the benefit of the offender but also for the well-being of the forgiver.

Holding onto resentment, anger, and bitterness can poison the soul and corrode the bonds of intimacy and trust within marriage. In Matthew 6:14-15, Jesus warns, "For if you forgive other people when they sin against you, your heavenly Father will also forgive you. But if you do not forgive others their sins, your Father will not forgive your sins."

This passage underscores the interconnectedness of forgiveness and spiritual well-being, highlighting the importance of releasing the burden of unforgiveness in order to experience the fullness of God's grace and mercy in our own lives.

Moreover, forgiveness is not a one-time event but a process that unfolds over time. It requires a willingness to let go of the desire for revenge or retribution and instead extend grace and mercy to the one who has wronged us.

Romans 12:19-21 admonishes, "Do not take revenge, my dear friends, but leave room for God's wrath, for it is written: 'It is mine to avenge; I will repay,' says the Lord. On the contrary: 'If your enemy is hungry, feed him; if he is thirsty, give him something to drink. In doing this, you will heap burning coals on his head.' Do not be overcome by evil, but overcome evil with good."

This passage reminds us that forgiveness is ultimately an act of liberation – freeing us from the bondage of bitterness and resentment and allowing us to move forward with a spirit of grace and compassion.

In the context of marriage, forgiveness is essential for cultivating a relationship characterized by love, trust, and intimacy.

When conflicts arise and mistakes are made as they inevitably will be the ability to extend and receive forgiveness is essential for maintaining a strong and healthy bond between spouses. 1 Peter 4:8 encourages us to "Above all, love each other deeply, because love covers over a multitude of sins."

This verse speaks to the power of love to transcend and transform even the most grievous offenses, offering a path to reconciliation and restoration.

Forgiveness is also a process of healing and restoration, both individually and within the marriage relationship.

As we release the burden of unforgiveness and extend grace to our spouses, we create space for healing and renewal to take place. Isaiah 43:18-19 declares, "Forget the former things; do not dwell on the past. See, I am doing a new thing! Now it springs up; do you not perceive it? I am making a way in the wilderness and streams in the wasteland."

This passage reminds us that forgiveness opens the door to new possibilities and fresh beginnings, allowing God to work miracles of restoration and redemption in our lives and marriages.

In conclusion, forgiveness is a transformative act that has the power to heal wounds, mend brokenness, and restore relationships to wholeness. In the context of marriage, forgiveness is essential for cultivating a relationship characterized by love, trust, and intimacy.

By extending and receiving forgiveness with kindness and compassion, couples can experience the fullness of God's grace and mercy in their lives and marriages, paving the way for healing, renewal, and restoration.

As we embrace the transformative power of forgiveness, we open our hearts to a future filled with hope, reconciliation, and love.

Chapter 5:

Cultivating Intimacy and Connection

Objectives:

1. Strengthen Emotional Bond: Explore ways to deepen emotional closeness between spouses, fostering better understanding and connection.

- 1 Peter 3:7
- Song of Solomon 5:16

2. Enhance Physical Intimacy: Discuss methods to improve physical closeness within marriage, nurturing affection and intimacy.

- 1 Corinthians 7:3-5

Goals:

1. Deepen Relationship: Offer practical tips for couples to build a stronger and more fulfilling bond.

- Ecclesiastes 4:9-10

Definition:

"Cultivating Intimacy and Connection" means actively working to strengthen both emotional and physical closeness in marriage, leading to a more fulfilling relationship.

∞∞∞

At the core of every thriving marriage lies intimacy a deep, soulful connection that encompasses emotional, physical, and spiritual dimensions.

Yet, amidst the turmoil of marital pain, intimacy can often feel elusive, overshadowed by hurt, resentment, and discord. In this chapter, we embark on a journey of exploration, uncovering practical strategies for cultivating intimacy and connection with your spouse, drawing from both timeless biblical principles and insights from modern relationship research.

Emotional intimacy forms the foundation of a healthy marriage, fostering trust, vulnerability, and mutual understanding between spouses. Proverbs 17:17 reminds us that "a friend loves at all times, and a brother is born for a time of adversity."

Cultivating friendship within marriage involves prioritizing quality time together, engaging in meaningful conversations, and actively listening to one another's thoughts and feelings.

By nurturing a deep, emotional bond with your spouse, you lay the groundwork for greater intimacy and connection.

Effective communication is essential for fostering emotional intimacy within marriage. In James 1:19, we are exhorted to be "quick to listen, slow to speak, and slow to become angry."

Communication involves more than just words it requires empathy, attentiveness, and a willingness to truly understand and validate your spouse's perspective. By practicing active listening and expressing empathy and compassion, you create a safe and nurturing environment where emotional intimacy can flourish.

Physical intimacy is another vital aspect of marriage, providing a unique opportunity for spouses to express their love and affection for one another. 1 Corinthians 7:3-5 highlights the importance of mutual respect and consideration in the marital relationship: "The husband should fulfill his marital duty to his wife, and likewise the wife to her husband.

The wife does not have authority over her own body but yields it to her husband. In the same way, the husband does not have authority over his own body but yields it to his wife.

Do not deprive each other except perhaps by mutual consent and for a time, so that you may devote yourselves to prayer. Then come together again so that Satan will not tempt you because of your lack of self-control." By prioritizing physical intimacy and affection within marriage, couples can strengthen their bond and enhance their emotional connection.

Spiritual intimacy is the cornerstone of a Christ-centered marriage, fostering a deep sense of unity and purpose between spouses. Ecclesiastes 4:12 declares, "Though one may be overpowered, two can defend themselves. A cord of three strands is not quickly broken."

By inviting God into the center of your marriage, you invite His presence, His guidance, and His love to permeate every aspect of your relationship. Engaging in spiritual practices such as prayer, worship, and Bible study together can deepen your spiritual connection and draw you closer to one another and to God.

Forgiveness is essential for cultivating intimacy and connection within marriage. Colossians 3:13 reminds us to "forgive one another if any of you has a grievance against someone. Forgive as the Lord forgave you."

When conflicts arise and mistakes are made, extending forgiveness to your spouse opens the door to reconciliation, healing, and renewed intimacy. By letting go of resentment and embracing grace, you create space for intimacy to thrive and flourish within your marriage.

Finally, prioritizing self-care and personal growth is crucial for cultivating intimacy and connection within marriage. Psalm 139:23-24 encourages us to "Search me, God, and know my heart; test me and know my anxious thoughts. See if there is any offensive way in me, and lead me in the way everlasting."

By investing in your own emotional, physical, and spiritual well-being, you become better equipped to show up fully present and engaged in your marriage, fostering deeper intimacy and connection with your spouse.

In conclusion, cultivating intimacy and connection within marriage is a lifelong journey that requires intentionality, effort, and commitment.

By prioritizing emotional, physical, and spiritual intimacy, practicing effective communication, extending forgiveness, and prioritizing personal growth, couples can strengthen their bond and create a marriage that is characterized by deep love, trust, and mutual respect

As they draw closer to one another and to God, they will discover a richness and depth of intimacy that will sustain them through the trials and triumphs of married life.

Chapter 8:

Embracing Growth and Transformation

Objectives:

1. Encourage Personal Growth: Show how challenges in marriage can lead to personal growth and resilience.
- Romans 5:3-4
- James 1:2-4

2. Promote Adaptability: Discuss the importance of adapting to change and learning from experiences for a stronger marriage.
- Proverbs 3:5-6
- Isaiah 43:18-19

Goals:

1. Inspire Reflection: Encourage readers to see marital challenges as opportunities for personal growth.

• Philippians 3:13-14

2. Facilitate Change: Offer practical advice on embracing change for a thriving marriage.

     • 2 Corinthians 3:18

Definition:

"Embracing Growth and Transformation" means seeing marriage challenges as chances to grow personally and together, leading to positive changes in the relationship.

∞ ∞ ∞

Marriage is not merely a destination but a journey a journey of growth, transformation, and discovery.

Along the way, couples encounter both joys and sorrows, triumphs and trials, but it is through these experiences that they are shaped and refined into the people they are meant to be.

In this final chapter, we reflect on the lessons learned from the pain of marriage and how it can ultimately lead to greater wisdom, compassion, and resilience. With faith as our guide, we embark on a journey of healing and renewal.

Pain has a way of revealing our vulnerabilities, exposing the cracks and fractures in our relationships that we may have overlooked or ignored.

Yet, it is through these moments of struggle and adversity that we are given an opportunity for growth and transformation. James 1:2-4 reminds us, "Consider it pure joy, my brothers and sisters, whenever you face trials of many kinds, because you know that the testing of your faith produces perseverance. Let perseverance finish its work so that you may be mature and complete, not lacking anything." In the crucible of pain, we are refined like gold, emerging stronger, wiser, and more resilient than before.

One of the greatest lessons that pain teaches us is the importance of humility and vulnerability within marriage.

It is easy to become prideful and defensive when faced with challenges, but true growth requires a willingness to admit our faults, acknowledge our weaknesses, and seek forgiveness when needed. 1 Peter 5:5-6 reminds us, "All of you, clothe yourselves with humility toward one another, because, 'God opposes the proud but shows favor to the humble.' Humble yourselves, therefore, under God's mighty hand, that he may lift you up in due time."

By embracing humility and vulnerability, couples create a culture of grace and acceptance within their marriage, fostering deeper intimacy and connection with one another.

Moreover, pain has a way of deepening our capacity for empathy and compassion towards others. As we walk through our own struggles and experience the healing power of grace and forgiveness, we are better equipped to extend the same to those around us. 2 Corinthians 1:3-4 reminds us, "Praise be to the God and Father of our Lord Jesus Christ, the Father of compassion and the God of all comfort, who comforts us in all our troubles, so that we can comfort those in any trouble with the comfort we ourselves receive from God."

By allowing our own experiences of pain and healing to shape us, we become vessels of hope and healing for others who are walking a similar journey.

Furthermore, pain can serve as a catalyst for personal and relational transformation, prompting us to reevaluate our priorities, values, and goals within marriage. Romans 12:2 exhorts us, "Do not conform to the pattern of this world, but be transformed by the renewing of your mind. Then you will be able to test and approve what God's will is his good, pleasing and perfect will."

In the midst of pain, couples are invited to surrender their own agendas and desires to God's perfect plan for their marriage, trusting in His faithfulness and provision every step of the way.

Ultimately, the journey of growth and transformation within marriage is a lifelong process, requiring patience, perseverance, and a willingness to embrace change. Philippians 1:6 assures us, "being confident of this, that he who began a good work in you will carry it on to completion until the day of Christ Jesus."

As couples lean into the pain of marriage with faith and resilience, they can trust that God is at work behind the scenes, weaving together a beautiful tapestry of redemption and renewal.

In conclusion, the pain of marriage is not the end of the story but rather the beginning of a new chapter a chapter of growth, transformation, and renewal. Through humility, empathy, and a willingness to embrace change, couples can emerge from their struggles stronger, wiser, and more deeply connected than before.

With faith as our guide and love as our compass, we embark on a journey of healing and transformation, trusting in God's faithfulness to lead us every step of the way.

Epilogue: Hope for the Journey Ahead

As we draw the final pages of this book to a close, it's important to recognize that the journey of marriage is not a solitary one.

It's a shared voyage, filled with peaks of joy and valleys of pain, where two souls navigate the waters of life together. Yet, amidst the challenges and struggles, there is always hope hope for healing, hope for renewal, and hope for a brighter future.

For many men, the pain of marriage can feel isolating, overwhelming, and at times, insurmountable. It's a weight they carry in the depths of their hearts, often hidden from the outside world behind a mask of stoicism and strength. But the truth is, they are not alone.

There is a community of support waiting to walk alongside them, offering a listening ear, a helping hand, and a word of encouragement when needed most.

At the heart of this book lies a message of hope for the journey ahead, hope for transformation, and hope for a thriving and fulfilling marriage. With faith as our guide and love as our compass, we embark on a journey of healing and renewal, trusting in God's faithfulness to lead us every step of the way.

For those who find themselves in the midst of marital pain, know that there is light at the end of the tunnel.

The pain you are experiencing is not the end of the story but merely a chapter in a much larger narrative.

It's a chapter filled with lessons to be learned, growth to be experienced, and grace to be extended. And though the road ahead may be long and difficult, it is a road worth traveling, for it leads to a place of healing, restoration, and renewed intimacy with your spouse.

But healing and renewal do not come without effort. They require a willingness to confront the pain of the past, to lean into vulnerability and humility, and to embrace change with open arms.

It's a journey that requires courage, perseverance, and a willingness to seek help when needed. Whether it's through prayer, counseling, or support groups, there are resources available to help you navigate the complexities of marriage and find healing and restoration along the way.

As we close this book, let us remember that no matter how deep the pain may be, there is always hope. Hope for a brighter tomorrow, hope for a stronger marriage, and hope for a future filled with love, joy, and fulfillment.

May this book serve as a beacon of hope and encouragement on your journey toward a thriving and fulfilling marriage. And may you always remember that with faith, perseverance, and a willingness to seek help when needed, anything is possible.

So, as you turn the page to the next chapter of your marriage, do so with courage, with hope, and with a steadfast belief that the best is yet to come.

For the journey ahead may be challenging, but it is also filled with endless possibilities for growth, transformation, and joy. And as you walk hand in hand with your spouse, may you always remember that you are not alone for God is with you, guiding you, and sustaining you every step of the way.

Acknowledgement

First and foremost, I am profoundly grateful to God for His unwavering guidance and grace throughout the writing of this book. His wisdom and love have been the cornerstone of my journey, and I am humbled by His presence in every step of this process.

To my beloved spouse, thank you for your endless support, understanding, and patience. Your love and encouragement have been my strength, and your willingness to walk this journey with me has been an invaluable source of inspiration.

I extend my heartfelt thanks to my family and friends who have provided encouragement, prayers, and understanding. Your support has been a beacon of light, especially during the challenging moments of writing this book.

A special thank you to my editor, [Editor's Name], for your keen insights, meticulous attention to detail, and unwavering dedication to helping this book reach its full potential. Your expertise and guidance have been indispensable.

To the members of our church community and all those who have shared their personal stories and experiences, thank you for your openness and trust. Your journeys have enriched this book and provided a deeper understanding of the complexities of marriage.

I am also grateful to the scholars, pastors, and counselors whose work and teachings have profoundly influenced this book. Your dedication to understanding and teaching the principles of healthy, faith-based relationships has been an invaluable resource.

To my readers, thank you for taking the time to embark on this journey with me. Your willingness to explore the depths of marital pain and seek healing through biblical wisdom is both humbling and inspiring. I pray that this book serves as a source of hope, encouragement, and transformation in your lives.

Finally, I would like to acknowledge everyone who has played a part, whether directly or indirectly, in the creation of this book. Your contributions, no matter how small, have made a significant impact on bringing this project to fruition.

With deepest gratitude,

Pastor Muzi Khumalo

About The Author

Pastor Muzi Khumalo

Pastor Muzi M Khumalo epitomizes an enthusiastic and visionary leader, driven by a profound commitment to delivering a message of reconciliation to the world. Rooted in his fervent dedication to preaching, teaching, and exemplifying Christlikeness, Pastor Khumalo draws inspiration from 2 Corinthians 5:1-20, where the transformative power of reconciliation is vividly portrayed.

With an extensive tenure of ministry experience under his belt, Pastor Khumalo embarked on a journey of scholarly enrichment, obtaining a Diploma in Bible and Theology from the esteemed Eswatini College of Theology. This academic pursuit not only honed his theological acumen but also equipped him with the tools necessary to effectively convey the timeless truths of Scripture.

As a testament to his commitment to collaborative ministry and fellowship, Pastor Khumalo proudly aligns himself with the Christian Leaders Fellowship (CLF), a network dedicated to fostering unity and cooperation among Christian leaders worldwide.

Currently, Pastor Khumalo serves under the esteemed leadership of Apostle T. Dlamini at God's Voice International Church, Eswatini, where he diligently labors to fulfill his calling and advance the kingdom of God.